20

Let's Explore
Technology

by Joe Levit

BUMBA BOOKS™

LERNER PUBLICATIONS ◆ MINNEAPOLIS

Note to Educators

Throughout this book, you'll find critical-thinking questions. These can be used to engage young readers in thinking critically about the topic and in using the text and photos to do so.

Lerner Publications Company
A division of Lerner Publishing Group, Inc.
241 First Avenue North
Minneapolis, MN 55401 USA

For reading levels and more information, look up this title at www.lernerbooks.com.

Library of Congress Cataloging-in-Publication Data

Names: Levit, Joseph, author.
Title: Let's explore technology / by Joe Levit.
Description: Minneapolis : Lerner Publications, [2018] | Series: Bumba books. A first look at STEM | Includes
    bibliographical references and index. | Audience: Ages 4–7.
Identifiers: LCCN 2017049725 (print) | LCCN 2017057667 (ebook) | ISBN 9781541507845 (eb pdf) |
    ISBN 9781541503267 (lb : alk. paper) | ISBN 9781541527027 (pb : alk. paper)
Subjects: LCSH: Technology—Juvenile literature.
Classification: LCC T48 (ebook) | LCC T48 .L435 2018 (print) | DDC 600—dc23

LC record available at https://lccn.loc.gov/2017049725

Manufactured in the United States of America
1-43821-33654-12/21/2017

Table of Contents

What Is Technology?

Technology uses science to

make life easier.

People use technology to

create objects.

These objects are inventions.

Technology helps people do big jobs. A lawn mower cuts the grass.

What other big jobs can technology help us do?

Technology saves time.

A dishwasher cleans many

dishes at once.

Why do people want to save time?

We use umbrellas
when it is raining.
They keep us from
getting wet.

Technology gets people from one

place to another.

People drive cars and ride bikes.

They ride in airplanes and trains.

Phones let us talk to people

who are far away.

We can take pictures with

cell phones.

Computers hold information.

They can quickly solve

math problems.

Computers also help create

new technology.

How else do people use computers?

Technology helps us every day.

It is always changing.

Look at the technology all around you.

Technology helps solve problems.

Think about an object that could

make your life easier.

Then create an invention!

Useful Inventions

cell phone

car

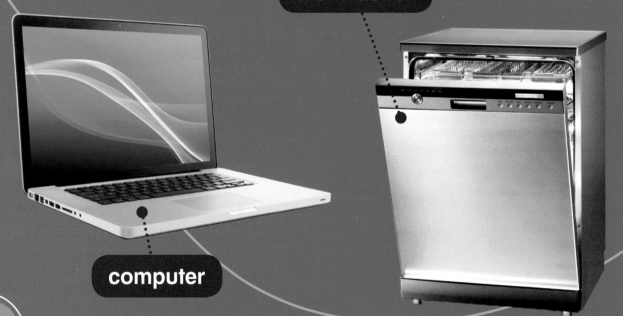

dishwasher

computer

Picture Glossary

computer

a machine that
stores information

invention

a new object or way
of doing something

science

learning about
the world

solve

find an answer

Read More

Ripley, Catherine. *Why? The Best Ever Question and Answer Book about Nature, Science and the World around You.* Berkeley, CA: Owlkids Books, 2018.

Silverman, Buffy. *How Do Trains Work?* Minneapolis: Lerner Publications, 2016.

Worth, Bonnie. *Oh, the Things They Invented! All about Great Inventors.* New York: Random House, 2015.

Index

Photo Credits

The images in this book are used with the permission of: © Amy Salveson/Independent Picture Service (lawn mower design element); Nestor Rizhniak/Shutterstock.com, p. 5; Elena Elisseeva/Shutterstock.com, pp. 6–7; Sergey Novikov/Shutterstock.com, p. 8; Michael C. Gray/Shutterstock.com, pp. 10–11; wavebreakmedia/Shutterstock.com, pp. 13, 16–17; LightField Studios/Shutterstock.com, p. 14; Dmytro Zinkevych/Shutterstock.com, pp. 19, 21; REDPIXEL.PL/Shutterstock.com, p. 22 (top left); Rawpixel.com/Shutterstock.com, p. 22 (top right); ifong/Shutterstock.com, p. 22 (bottom left); Pro3DArtt/Shutterstock.com, p. 22 (bottom right); Billion Photos/Shutterstock.com, p. 23 (top left); Vitalliy/Shutterstock.com, p. 23 (top right); Creativa Images/Shutterstock.com, p. 23 (bottom left).

Front cover: YAKOBCHUK VIACHESLAV/Shutterstock.com.